BAKING
with kids

THANKS TO
AGNES
ALEX
BAILEY
CHRISTIAN
ED
KARIN
LINNEA
LOVISA
LUDVIG
MABEY
MARIE
MASSAR
MIRA
NIKE
NILS
NORA
PAULINA
PHILIP
ROSSO
RUTH
SIGNE
TOMAS
ALCRO
SMEG

Good
Baking
Tools

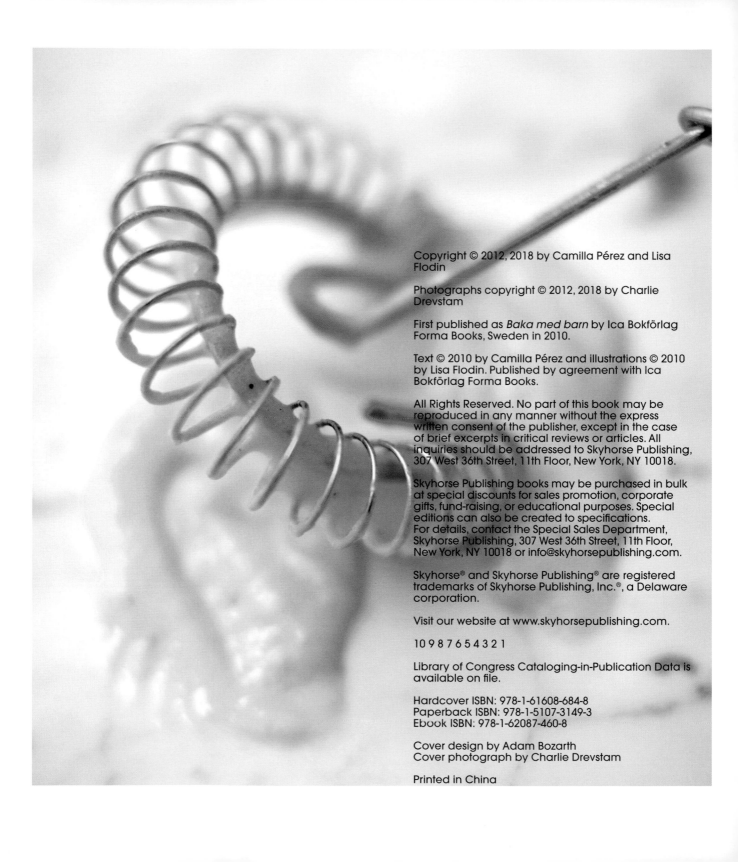

Skyhorse Publishing books may be purchased in bulk at special discounts for sales promotion, corporate gifts, fund-raising, or educational purposes. Special editions can also be created to specifications. For details, contact the Special Sales Department, Skyhorse Publishing, 307 West 36th Street, 11th Floor, New York, NY 10018 or info@skyhorsepublishing.com.

Skyhorse® and Skyhorse Publishing® are registered trademarks of Skyhorse Publishing, Inc.®, a Delaware corporation.

Visit our website at www.skyhorsepublishing.com.

10 9 8 7 6 5 4 3 2 1

Library of Congress Cataloging-in-Publication Data is available on file.

Hardcover ISBN: 978-1-61608-684-8
Paperback ISBN: 978-1-5107-3149-3
Ebook ISBN: 978-1-62087-460-8

Cover design by Adam Bozarth
Cover photograph by Charlie Drevstam

Printed in China

BAKING
with kids

Inspiring a Love of Cooking with Recipes for Bread, Cupcakes, Cheesecake, and More!

CAMILLA PÉREZ and **LISA FLODIN**

PHOTOGRAPHY BY
Charlie Drevstam

Skyhorse Publishing

One of the sweetest sensory experiences is the smell of freshly baked goods. It brings us pleasure and warmth, and it is something that both children and adults associate with comfort and joy.

This book is a helpful tool for kids who want to bake on their own, or accompanied by an adult. The rule of thumb is that the younger the baker, the more likely adult help will be required. The recipes were selected by taking what children love and appreciate into consideration, but also for the purpose of offering a wide array of baking options. There are both breads and pastries, and no prior baking experience is required. The book is filled with straightforward instructions that make baking an easy-to-do learning experience.

When children bake, they develop their dexterity and creativity, in addition to an interest in home-baked bread that is free of unnecessary additives. Best of all is the satisfaction of eating your very own creations …

AUTHOR & STYLIST CAMILLA PÉREZ
PHOTO CHARLIE DREVSTAM
GRAPHIC DESIGN & IDEA LISA FLODIN
BAKER CAMILLA SANDIN

CONTENTS

Standard U.S. to Metric Conversions

Ounces to grams:
0.9 oz = 25.5 g
1 oz = 28 g
1.8 oz = 51 g
3.5 oz = 99 g
5.3 oz = 150 g
7 oz = 198.5 g
10 oz = ¼ kg

Cups to liters/tablespoons (liquid):
⅕ cup = 3 ⅓ tbs
⅖ cup = 6 ⅓ tbs
⅗ cup = 9 ½ tbs
1 ⅓ cups = ⅓ liter
1 ¾ cups = ⅖ liter
2 cups = ½ liter

Cups to grams (solid—flour):
⅕ cup = 25 g
⅓ cup = 40 g
¾ cup = 85 g
1 cup = 110 g
1 ¾ cups = 195 g
2 cups = 220 g
3 cups = 330 g
4 cups = 440 g
5 cups = 550 g

Cups to grams (solid—sugar):
⅕ cup = 50 g
½ cup = 115 g
¾ cup = 170 g
1 cup = 225 g
2 cups (granulated) = 450 g
2 cups (powdered) = 250 g

For all other conversion needs, please visit the following websites:

www.metric-conversions.org/
www.recipegoldmine.com/kitchart/kitchart2.html

Good Baking Habits
...for kids

- **Always begin by asking an adult** if you can use the kitchen and make sure that they can assist you if you need them.

- **Wash your hands** with soap and water before you begin.

- **Always read the entire recipe before you begin,** and follow the recipe as accurately as possible to achieve the best possible result.

- **Make sure you have all the ingredients** needed for the recipe before you begin. Place the ingredients on the counter so that you can see them, to ensure that you have them all.

- **Make sure you have a good baking surface,** such as a table at a good working height. Use a stool or chair if you need to. Carefully clean the baking table before you begin.

- **Use oven mitts or a pot holder** when opening the oven.

- **Always clean up** in the kitchen when you are done.

- **Make your family and friends happy** by treating them to your baked goods.

- **You can keep baked goods in the freezer for months.** The less fat (butter and oil) you use in the recipe, the longer the goods will last in the freezer.

EXPLANATIONS

½ = half

approx = approximately (more or less)

decorate = to make something beautiful with nice things

lukewarm = when you feel the temperature with your finger and it does not feel warm or cold

oz = ounce(s)

bake = to cook something in the oven

rise/ferment = allow the dough to grow bigger (it grows from the gas building up inside the dough) with yeast or a leavening agent such as baking powder

a pinch = usually used with spices, literally when you grab a pinch of the spice between your index finger and your thumb

tbsp = tablespoon

measure = measure the correct quantity of an ingredient by using a measure, such as a cup

butter and flour = greasing the inside of a baking pan with butter and sprinkling with flour or breadcrumbs, to prevent the cake from sticking to the pan

turn out the cake = place a plate on top of the cake pan and turn it upside down

tsp = teaspoon

whisk = this is done with an electric mixer or with a hand whisk to trap air inside the liquid

bread fun

Rose Hip Bread

These beautiful breads will attract hungry gazes, thanks to the red flour. Serve with butter.

20 pieces
You'll Need
1.8 OZ BUTTER (ROOM TEMPERATURE)
0.9 OZ YEAST (½ PACKAGE)
2 CUPS WATER
⅕ CUP ROSE HIP SHELL FLOUR
4 ⅕-4 ⅗ CUPS WHEAT FLOUR
⅕ CUP LIGHT SYRUP
½ TBSP SALT
1 ⁹⁄₁₀ CUPS SPELT FLOUR

2.

4.

1. Take the butter out of the fridge to bring it to a nice room temperature.

2. Crumble the yeast into a bowl.

3. Measure the water and heat it to about 98.6 degrees (lukewarm) in a saucepan or in the microwave. Pour the water over the yeast in the bowl and stir with a spoon until the yeast has dissolved.

4. Measure the remaining ingredients and pour them into the bowl. Stir, and knead into a dough for at least 10 minutes by hand, or 8 minutes if you are using a machine.

5. Cover the bowl with a clean kitchen towel and let the dough rise for 30 minutes.

6. Cover 2 baking sheets with parchment paper.

7. Sprinkle flour over the work surface and place the dough on the table.

8. Divide the dough into 4 equal parts with a knife. Then divide each part into 5 equal parts so that you have a total of 20 parts. Shape the pieces into round balls. Then press lightly on either side of each one until it looks like an oval bun with two pointy ends.

9. Place the breads on the parchment paper on the baking sheets and cover them with clean kitchen towels. Allow them to rise for 40 minutes.

10. Heat the oven to 425 degrees.

11. Place one baking sheet at a time in the middle of the oven and bake the breads for about 8 minutes. Keep an eye on them to make sure that they turn a nice golden color without getting burned. Remove the baking sheets and place the breads on a wire rack and cover them with a kitchen towel while they cool off. Store the breads in plastic bags.

7.

You can make your own hearty variation of the classical french baguette. This baguette gets a lovely crispy shell.

3 baguettes
You'll Need:
0.9 OZ YEAST

2 CUPS WATER

2 CUPS COARSE RYE FLOUR

4 ⅓ CUPS WHEAT FLOUR

½ TBSP SALT

1.8 OZ BUTTER (ROOM TEMPERATURE)

1. **Take out the butter so that it softens.** Crumble the yeast into a bowl.

2. **Heat water in a saucepan** or in the microwave to about 98.6 degrees (lukewarm)

3. **Pour about ⅖ cup of water over the yeast in the bowl** and stir with a spoon until the yeast has dissolved. Pour in the remaining water and stir a little bit more.

4. **Measure the rest of the ingredients** and pour them into the bowl. Mix into a dough. Knead the dough for 12 minutes by hand, or 8 minutes if you are using a bread maker.

5. **Cover the bowl with a clean kitchen towel** and let the dough rise for 30 minutes.

6. **Sprinkle a little bit of wheat flour onto the work surface** and place the dough on it. Divide the dough into 3 equal parts.

7. **Roll the pieces into long baguettes.** Press a little bit of coarse rye flour on top of the baguettes and place them on parchment paper on a baking sheet. Place a kitchen towel over the baguettes and let them rise for 45 minutes.

8. **Heat the oven to 475 degrees.**

9. **Place the baking sheet in the middle of the oven** and bake for about 18 minutes, until the baguettes have a nice color. Remove the baking sheet from the oven and place the baguettes on a wire rack. Cover with a kitchen towel and let them cool off. Store the baguettes in plastic bags.

hearty baguette

APPLE BUNS

Delicious buns with delectable filling
that are excellent for snack-time.

1. **Crumble the yeast** into a bowl.

2. **Melt the butter** in a saucepan.

3. **Measure the milk** and pour it into the pan. Heat the liquid to about 98.6 degrees (lukewarm). Pour about ⅖ cup of the liquid over the yeast in the bowl and stir with a spoon until the yeast has dissolved. Add the rest of the liquid and stir some more.

4. **Crack the egg** against the edge of the bowl and pour it into the bowl.

5. **Measure the flour, salt, and sugar**, and pour them into the bowl. Stir.

6. **Knead the dough** for at least 10 minutes by hand, or 8 minutes in the bread maker.

7. **Sprinkle some flour onto the work surface** and place the dough on the table.

8. **Divide the dough into 4 equal parts.** Then divide each part into 4 equal parts so that you end up with 16 pieces.

9. **Shape the dough into round balls** and place them on parchment paper on 2 baking sheets.

10. **Place clean kitchen towels over the buns** and allow them to rise for 30 minutes.

11. **You can mix** the cinnamon and the applesauce for the filling while the dough is rising.

12. **Carefully press with your fingers** to create a hollow in each bun and put a big teaspoon of filling into each cavity.

13. **Heat the oven to 475 degrees.**

14. **Crack an egg into a cup** and lightly whisk it with a fork. Carefully brush the buns with the beaten egg. Use a bread brush, and avoid brushing the filling.

15. **Place the baking sheets**, one at a time, in the middle of the oven and bake for about 7 minutes until the buns are golden brown. Take out the baking sheets and place kitchen towels over the buns until they have cooled off.

16. **Store the apple buns** in plastic bags.

16 buns

You'll Need:
1.8 OZ YEAST
5.3 OZ BUTTER
1 ⅓ CUPS MILK
1 EGG
4 ⅗ CUPS WHEAT FLOUR
½ TSP SALT
⅕ CUP RAW SUGAR
1 EGG FOR BRUSHING

Filling:
⅖ CUP LIGHTLY SUGA-
   RED APPLE SAUCE
1 TSP CINNAMON

9.

11.

12.

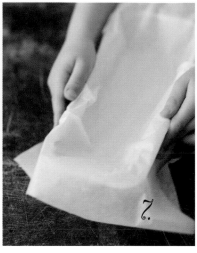

A succulent and filling bread that is packed with nutrition and energy. And it is a piece of cake to make if you have all the ingredients at home.

Fruit Bread

1. Heat the oven to 350 degrees.

2. Measure all the dry ingredients and the chopped fruit and pour them into a bowl, except for the seeds that are going on top of the bread. Stir with a spoon.

3. Measure the yogurt and pour it into the bowl.

4. Measure the syrup and pour it into the bowl.

5. Mix everything into a batter.

6. Grate the unpeeled apple, except for the core, with a grater and stir it into the batter.

7. Press parchment paper into a bread pan and cut any excessive paper if it is bigger than the pan.

8. Pour the batter into the pan.

9. Sprinkle the seeds over the batter.

10. Put the pan onto a baking sheet and place the sheet in the lower part of the oven. Bake the bread for 1 hour and 20 minutes. Check the bread with a cake tester. If it comes out sticky, the bread is not quite finished yet. Then test the bread every 5 minutes until the cake tester comes out dry and clean.

11. Remove the baking sheet with the bread and allow it to cool off a little bit before you carefully remove it from the pan. Store the bread in a plastic bag.

1 loaf
You'll Need:
- ⁴/₅ CUP OATS
- 2 CUPS SIFTED SPELT FLOUR
- ²/₅ CUP FLAX SEEDS
- ²/₅ CUP DRIED APRICOTS, CHOPPED OR ²/₅ CUP DRIED MIXED FRUIT, CHOPPED
- ¹/₅ CUP SUNFLOWER SEEDS
- 2 TSP BAKING SODA
- 1 PINCH OF SALT
- 1 ¾ CUPS PLAIN YOGURT
- 3 TBSP DARK BREAD SYRUP
- 1 APPLE
- 2 TBSP MIXED SEEDS FOR GARNISH. THE MIX YOU SEE IN THE PICTURE CONSISTS OF 1 TBSP PUMPKIN SEEDS, ½ TBSP FLAX SEEDS, AND ½ TBSP POPPY SEEDS, BUT YOU CAN USE ANY SEEDS YOU WANT.

healthy
croissants

LUXURIOUS CROISSANTS THAT ARE EXCELLENT WHEN YOU WANT TO IMPRESS YOUR PARENTS OR ANYBODY ELSE. THEY ARE A LITTLE BIT HEALTHIER THAN THE USUAL CROISSANTS.

1. Crumble the yeast into a bowl. Melt the butter in a saucepan.

2. Measure the milk and pour it into the saucepan. Heat the liquid to about 98.6 degrees (lukewarm). Pour about ⅓ cup of the liquid over the yeast in the bowl and stir with a spoon until the yeast has dissolved. Add the remaining liquid and stir a little bit. Measure the salt, sugar, and flour, and pour them into the bowl.

3. Crack the eggs into a cup and pour them into the bowl.

4. Mix into a dough and knead it for 10 minutes by hand, or 8 minutes in a bread machine.

5. Cover the bowl with a clean kitchen towel and allow the dough to rise for 30 minutes.

6. Sprinkle flour over the work surface and place the dough on the table.

7. Roll out the dough into a rectangle, about ¼-inch thick.

8. Divide the dough with a knife into 8 squares. Then divide the squares on the diagonal into 16 triangles.

9. Roll the triangles, starting with the broadest part of the triangle, and tug at the corners lightly as you roll the triangles. Lightly bend the croissants at the corners to shape them into half moons. Place the croissants onto 2 baking sheets that have been covered with parchment paper and cover the croissants with clean kitchen towels. Allow them to rise for 30 minutes.

10. Heat the oven to 475 degrees.

11. Crack an egg into a cup and whisk it lightly with a fork. Brush the croissants with the egg using a bread brush.

12. Place one baking sheet at a time in the middle of the oven and bake for 7 minutes. Remove the croissants when they have a little bit of color. Place them on a wire rack and cover them with a kitchen towel until they have cooled off.

13. Store the croissants in plastic bags.

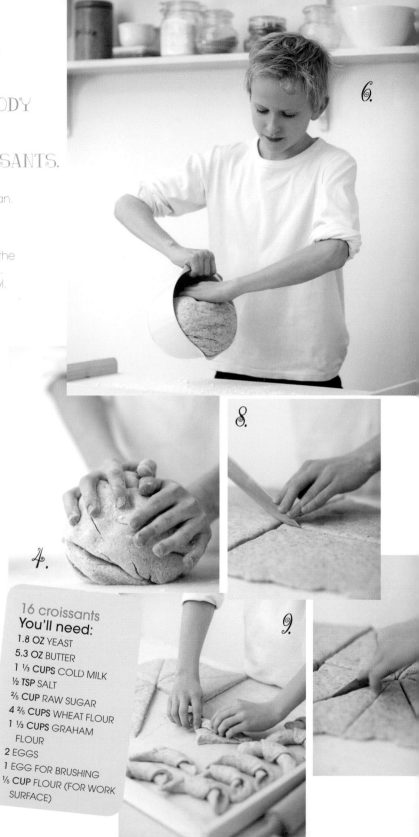

16 croissants
You'll need:
1.8 OZ YEAST
5.3 OZ BUTTER
1 ⅓ CUPS COLD MILK
½ TSP SALT
⅖ CUP RAW SUGAR
4 ⅖ CUPS WHEAT FLOUR
1 ⅓ CUPS GRAHAM FLOUR
2 EGGS
1 EGG FOR BRUSHING
⅕ CUP FLOUR (FOR WORK SURFACE)

LOAF

Most people enjoy a good loaf sandwich, and you can make lots of them out of this delicious loaf.

1. **Crumble the yeast into a bowl.**

2. **Heat the water in a saucepan** or in a microwave until it is about 98.6 degrees (lukewarm). Pour ⅕ cup of water over the yeast in the bowl and stir with a spoon until the yeast has dissolved. Add the rest of the liquid and stir a bit more.

3. **Pour the remaining ingredients** into the bowl and mix.

4. **Knead the dough for at least 12 minutes** by hand or 10 minutes if you are using a bread machine. Cover the bowl with a clean kitchen towel and let the dough rise for 30 minutes.

5. **Sprinkle flour over the work surface** and place the dough on it. Divide the dough into 3 equal parts and shape them into loaves.

6. **Place the loaves onto parchment paper** on a baking sheet and cover them with a kitchen towel again. Let the loaves rise for 30 minutes. Heat the oven to 350 degrees.

7. **Place the baking sheet** in the lower part of the oven and bake the loaves for about 25 minutes, until they have a nice color. Remove the sheet and place the loaves on a wire rack and cover them with a kitchen towel while they are cooling down. Store the loaves in plastic bags.

3 loafs
You'll need:
1.8 **OZ** YEAST

2 **CUPS** WATER

½ **TBSP** SALT

1 **OZ** BUTTER (ROOM TEMPERATURE)

1 **TSP** ANISE

1 **TSP** FENNEL

⅗ **CUP** DARK SYRUP

3 **CUPS** RYE FLOUR

4 ⅕ **CUPS** WHEAT FLOUR

A tasty roll is excellent at breakfast, at snack time, or during the evening meal. Home baked rolls taste absolutely delicious.

1. **Crumble the yeast into a bowl.**

2. **Melt the butter** in a saucepan.

3. **Measure the water and pour it into the saucepan.** Heat the liquid to about 98.6 degrees (lukewarm). Pour some of the liquid over the yeast in the bowl and stir with a spoon until the yeast has dissolved. Pour the rest of the liquid into the bowl and stir a bit more.

4. **Measure the remaining ingredients** and pour them into the bowl and stir.

5. **Knead into a dough for at least 10 minutes** by hand, or 8 minutes if you are using a bread machine.

6. **Sprinkle flour onto the work surface** and place the dough on the table.

7. **Divide the dough into 4 equal parts** with a knife; then divide each part into four equal parts, so that you have 16 pieces.

8. **Cover 2 baking sheets with baking paper.**

9. **Roll the pieces into round balls** and place them onto the baking sheets. Cover the rolls with a clean kitchen towel and let them rise for 1 hour.

10. **Preheat the oven to 435 degrees.**

11. **Remove the towel and place one sheet at a time in the middle of the oven.** Bake the bread about 8 minutes until it has a nice color.

12. **Remove the baking sheet and place the rolls on a wire rack.** Place a towel over the rolls and let them cool off before you store them in plastic bags.

16 rolls
You'll need:
1.8 **OZ** YEAST
1.8 **OZ** BUTTER
2 **CUPS** WATER
1/5 **CUP** LIGHT SYRUP
1 1/2 **TSP** SALT
4/5 **CUP** WHEAT GERM
3 2/5 **CUPS** RYE FLOUR
1 3/4 **CUPS** WHEAT FLOUR

30 grandma's rolls

Grandma's
Rolls

baking fun

Cupcakes
with Frosting

20 Cupcakes
You'll need:
0.9 OZ BUTTER
3/5 CUP SUNFLOWER OR RAPESEED OIL
1 CUP GRANULATED SUGAR
3 EGGS
2 CUPS FLOUR
1 TBSP VANILLA SUGAR
2 TSP BAKING POWDER
2/5 CUP MILK
AMERICAN MUFFIN CUPS

The frosting makes the cupcakes extra beautiful and tasty. Use your imagination and your favorite candy to create your own pieces of art. They make excellent gifts to give to someone special

1. Preheat the oven to 350 degrees.

2. Place 20 muffin cups onto 2 baking sheets.

3. Melt the butter in a saucepan or a microwave. Pour the butter into a bowl.

4. Measure the oil and pour it into the bowl.

5. Measure the granulated sugar and stir it into the bowl.

6. Beat with an electric mixer until you have a fluffy batter.

7. Crack the eggs into a cup and pour them into the bowl. Stir with a spatula.

8. Take out a new bowl.

9. Measure the flour, vanilla sugar, and baking powder, and pour them into the empty bowl. Stir them together with a spoon and pour the flour mixture into the bowl with the batter. Mix thoroughly with a spatula.

10. Measure the milk and stir it into the batter with a spatula.

11. Pour the batter into the muffin cups using a spoon. The batter should fill half of the muffin cups. If you have any empty muffin cups left over, remove them from the baking sheet.

12. Place one sheet at a time in the middle of the oven and bake for about 15 minutes. Use a cake tester to check if the muffins are ready—if the cake tester comes out a bit sticky, they are not quite ready. Check the cupcakes every two minutes until the cake tester comes out dry.

13. Remove the baking sheets from the oven and let the cupcakes cool off for at least 30 minutes if you are going to decorate them with frosting.

Frosting on the next page

Frosting

5.

6.

1. Take out the package of butter for a while before you make the frosting so that the butter softens and becomes easier to work with.

2. Place the butter in a bowl.

3. Add the powdered sugar to the bowl. Whisk together the butter and sugar with an electric mixer for about 2 minutes.

4. Add cream cheese to the bowl and stir with a spatula.

5. Cut a lemon in half with a knife. Squeeze the juice out of one of the halves with your hand into a bowl. Pour the lemon juice into the bowl and stir with a spatula until you have a

smooth batter. Pour the batter into several small bowls. Color the batter with food coloring. Feel free to experiment with different colors by adding two different colors to the same bowl.

6. Use a spoon to put the batter onto the cupcakes. If you want, you can decorate the cupcakes with banana chips, licorice laces, or sprinkles. It is easier than it looks!

7. Allow the frosting to solidify and store the cupcakes in a plastic jar with a lid in the refrigerator. The cupcakes should be eaten within a week.

frosting
You'll need:
3.5 OZ CREAM CHEESE, I.E.,
    PHILADELPHIA CHEESE
2 OZ BUTTER
2 CUPS POWDFRED SUGAR
JUICE FROM HALF A LEMON
FOOD COLORING IN
    DIFFERENT COLORS

You'll need:

2 EGGS
⅘ **CUP** DARK MUSCOVADO (SUGAR)
1 ⅓ **CUPS** FLOUR
1 TSP BAKING POWDER
1 TSP BAKING SODA
2 TSP VANILLA SUGAR
1 TSP CINNAMON
3.5 OZ DARK CHOCOLATE
2 BANANAS (RIPE)
⅕ **CUP** MILK
⅕ **CUP** SUNFLOWER OR RAPESEED OIL
⅕ **CUP** SHREDDED COCONUT FOR THE
    PAN, OR POWDERED SUGAR

Often a favorite fruit, the banana is absolutely delicious to add to cake recipes. Dark chocolate and flavorful sugar will make this cake even tastier.

BANANA CAKE

1. **Crack the eggs** into a cup and pour them into a bowl.

2. **Measure the sugar** and pour it into the bowl. Beat the eggs and the sugar with an electric mixer until you have a fluffy batter.

3. **Take out a bowl** and place a strainer over it. Sift all the dry ingredients into the bowl: flour, baking powder, baking soda, vanilla sugar, and cinnamon. Mix them with a spoon. Pour the mixture into a bowl with the egg batter and stir.

4. **Grate the chocolate** with a grater or with a peeler, and add the grated chocolate to the bowl with the batter.

5. **Mash the bananas** on a plate using a fork. Put the mashed bananas into the bowl. Stir with a spatula.

6. **Measure the milk and oil,** and pour them into the bowl. Stir with a spatula.

7. **Preheat the oven to 350 degrees.**

8. **Take out a springform pan,** about 9.5 inches in diameter, butter it, and sprinkle it with coconut.

9. **Pour the batter into the pan** and place it on a rack in the middle of the oven.

10. **Bake the cake for about 40 minutes.** Check the cake with a cake tester—if the cake tester comes out a bit sticky, the cake is not quite ready, but may take a few more minutes to bake.

11. **Remove the cake from the oven and allow it to cool.** Remove the edge from the springform pan and sprinkle the cake with icing sugar if you want before you serve it. A dollop of whipped cream is also a delicious addition.

YOU CAN EXCHANGE THE DARK MUSCOVADO SUGAR FOR LIGHT OR RAW SUGAR.

You'll need:
10 GRAHAM CRACKERS
⁴/₅ CUP BRAN FLAKES
3.5 OZ BUTTER
1 TBSP WHIPPING CREAM
10 OZ CREAM CHEESE, I.E.,
    PHILADELPHIA
1 CAN QUARK CHEESE,
    ABOUT 4.4 OZ
¾ CUP SUGAR
A PINCH OF SALT
1 TSP VANILLA SUGAR
3 EGGS
½ CAN QUARK CHEESE WITH
    2 TBSP ICING SUGAR, AND
    1 TBSP VANILLA SUGAR,
    STIRRED TOGETHER.

A yummy American classic that is excellent on special occasions. Serve it with fresh berries to make it extra luxurious.

1. Chop the graham crackers and the bran flakes into small crumbs. You can use a rolling pin. Pour the crumbs into a bowl.

2. Melt the butter in a saucepan, and pour the butter over the crumbs in the bowl.

3. Measure the cream , pour it into the bowl, and stir with a ladle.

4. Preheat the oven to 300 degrees.

5. Take out a springform pan, about 9.5 inches in diameter. Pour the breadcrumb batter into the pan and flatten into a thin crust.

6. Place the pan on a wire rack in the middle of the oven and bake for 14 minutes.

7. Remove the pan from the oven and allow it to cool off.

8. Take out a new bowl and add the cream cheese and the quark (without the vanilla flavor). Whisk by hand.

9. Measure the sugar, salt, and vanilla, and pour them into the bowl.

10. Crack the eggs into a cup and pour them into the bowl. Whisk a little longer.

11. Preheat the oven to 300 degrees again.

12. Pour the mixture over the bottom of the pan and spread it out with a spatula.

13. Place the pan on a wire rack in the center of the oven and bake for 30 minutes. Turn off the oven, open the oven door a bit, and let the cake remain in there for 30 minutes.

14. Move the cake to the refrigerator and let it become cold.

15. Take the cake out of the fridge and remove the edge from the springform pan. Spread the topping on the cake with a spatula or a knife and serve.

cheesecake

5.

A delicious little cookie that is impossible to stop eating once you have tasted a bite.

CARAMEL CUTS

1. Preheat the oven to 400 degrees.

2. **Measure all the ingredients** and pour them into a bowl. Knead everything together with your hands into a dough.

3. **Sprinkle flour on the work surface** and place the dough on it. Divide the dough into two equal parts and shape them into two coils that are almost as long as the longest side of the baking sheet.

4. **Cover a baking sheet with baking paper** and place the coils on it. Flatten them with your hands until they are half their thickness. Place the baking sheet in the center of the oven and bake for about 7 minutes, until the coils are golden brown. Remove the baking sheet from the oven and place it on the stove.

5. **Cut the lengths into cookies** with a knife before the dough solidifies, but be careful and remember that the baking sheet and the lengths are still warm. Cut the cakes at an angle to make them extra pretty. Allow them to cool and store them in a cookie jar.

About 35 pieces
You'll need:
3.5 OZ BUTTER (ROOM TEMPERATURE)
4/5 CUP FLOUR
1 TSP VANILLA SUGAR
1/2 CUP GRANULATED SUGAR
1/2 TBSP SYRUP
1 TSP BAKING SODA
1/5 CUP WHEAT FLOUR FOR THE BAKING SURFACE

Macaroons

3.

8.

11.

Store coconut in plastic bags or a jar.

12.

Delicious treats for anyone who loves coconut. Chocolate and coconut make an excellent combination, so feel free to dip these yummy treats in melted chocolate.

1. **Melt the butter** in a saucepan or in the microwave and let the butter cool down slightly.

2. **Take out a cheese grater** and use it to zest half a lemon. Select whatever part of the grater you wish to use, as long as the zest is in small pieces.

3. **Crack the eggs into a cup** and pour them into a bowl.

4. **Measure the sugar and coconut,** and place them in the bowl with the lemon peel. Pour the cooled-down butter over it. Mix together to form a batter, but do not whisk.

5. **Let the batter rest for 10 minutes** so that it swells a bit and becomes easier to shape.

6. **Preheat the oven to 400 degrees.**

7. **Cover a baking sheet** with parchment paper.

8. **Pick up dollops of batter** that are as large as you wish the macaroons to be. About 2 tablespoons for each macaroon is a good quantity.

9. **Place the baking sheet in the middle of the oven** for about 13 minutes until they have browned slightly, but make sure that they do not get burned. Remove the baking sheet from the oven and allow the macaroons to cool.

10. **If you want to dip the macaroons in chocolate you need to melt the chocolate first.** You can do it in the microwave by breaking a chocolate bar into pieces and placing them in a cup in the microwave; that will make it easy to melt.

11. **You can also melt chocolate in what is called a water bath.** You place a bowl, small saucepan, or something similar in a large saucepan that is filled with water. The small bowl/pan bathes in the water in the large saucepan. Break the chocolate into small pieces and place them in the small bowl/pan. Then place the big saucepan on the stove and turn it to the second highest heat. When the water becomes warm, the chocolate will melt. Make sure that no water or steam gets mixed in with the chocolate.

12. **Dip the bottom of each macaroon in the chocolate** and place on a new baking paper. Remember that chocolate hardens pretty fast; you may need to reheat the melted chocolate once to dip all of the macaroons.

You'll need:

1.8 OZ BUTTER
ZEST OF HALF A LEMON
2 EGGS
⅕ CUP GRANULATED SUGAR
⅕ CUP RAW SUGAR
7 OZ SHREDDED COCONUT
OPTIONAL 3.5 OZ DARK BAKING
   CHOCOLATE

A delicious and filling cake that can feed many mouths. Invite all your friends over for cake.

carrot cake
WITH ORANGE CREAM

Orange Cream

You'll need:
⅕ **CUP** WHIPPING CREAM
⅕ **CUP** QUARK
1 **TBSP** ICING SUGAR
JUICE FROM 1 ORANGE

Measure the cream and pour into a bowl. Whip the cream with an electric mixer or hand beater until it is fluffy. Size up the quark and icing sugar and pour into the bowl. Squeeze an orange with your hands and press the juice into a cup. Pour the juice in the bowl. Mix the ingredients with a spoon into a smooth paste. Pour cream in a bowl and set in the refrigerator for a while before serving.

1. Heat the oven to 350 degrees.

2. Measure the oil and the sugar and pour them into a bowl. Whisk with an electric whisk.

3. Crack the eggs into a cup and pour them into the bowl. Beat the batter with an electric whisk until it is light and fluffy.

4. Measure milk, cinnamon, nutmeg, baking powder, baking soda, and salt, and pour them into a new bowl. Stir with a spoon, and pour the mixture into the bowl with the batter.

5. Pour the shredded carrots and the orange zest into the bowl. Mix the batter thoroughly with a spatula.

6. Butter the baking pan (about 9.5 inches in diameter) and sprinkle it with breadcrumbs. Pour the batter into the pan, and put the pan on a wire rack in the lower part of the oven. Bake the cake for about 40 minutes. Use a cake tester to check if the cake is done. If the cake tester comes out a bit sticky, it is not quite ready; allow it to bake for a few more minutes until the stick comes out dry.

7. Remove the cake from the oven and turn it onto a plate. Allow the cake to cool before you cut it up for a taste. Serve the carrot cake with the orange cream for an extra delicious flavor.

3.

You'll need:
1 ⅓ **CUPS** SUNFLOWER OR RAPESEED OIL
2 **CUPS** GRANULATED SUGAR
5 **EGGS**
2 ⅘ **CUPS** WHEAT FLOUR
1 **TSP** CINNAMON
1 **PINCH** GRATED NUTMEG
1 **TSP** BAKING POWDER
1 **TSP** BAKING SODA
1 **PINCH** SALT
10 **OZ** FINELY GRATED CARROT
ZEST OF 1 ORANGE

About 20 pastries

You'll need:
⅕ **CUP** GRANULATED SUGAR
3.5 **OZ** BUTTER
1 ⅗ **CUPS** WHEAT FLOUR
½ **TSP** BAKING POWDER
1 **EGG**
PASTRY PANS

filling:
VANILLA CREAM
FRESH BERRIES

7.

Making your own pastries is such a luxury. These are made out of a delicious shortbread crust and they are excellent during the holidays or other festive occasions.

Berry Pastries

1. **Put the sugar and the butter** in a bowl and mix with a fork until soft.

2. **Measure the flour and the baking powder** and pour them into the bowl.

3. **Crack the egg** into a cup and pour it into the bowl.

4. **Stir the mixture into a dough.** Cover the dough in plastic and place it in the refrigerator for 30 minutes.

5. **Heat the oven to 400 degrees.**

6. **Sprinkle a little bit of wheat flour** onto the working table and put the dough on it.

7. **Roll the dough out carefully** so that it doesn't crack. It should be about $\frac{1}{10}$-inch thick. Use a glass

to create circle shapes. The circles should be slightly bigger than the baking pans. Carefully press the dough into the pans and cut off any excessive dough.

8. **Put the pans onto a baking sheet** and place the sheet in the middle of the oven. Bake for 6 minutes until the dough has a golden brown color. Remove the baking sheet from the oven and allow the cookies to rest for a few minutes before you remove them from the pans. It is best to do it when they are lukewarm. Allow the cookies to cool off on the table.

9. **Beat the vanilla cream** and add a dollop inside each cookie. Garnish with fresh berries.

8.

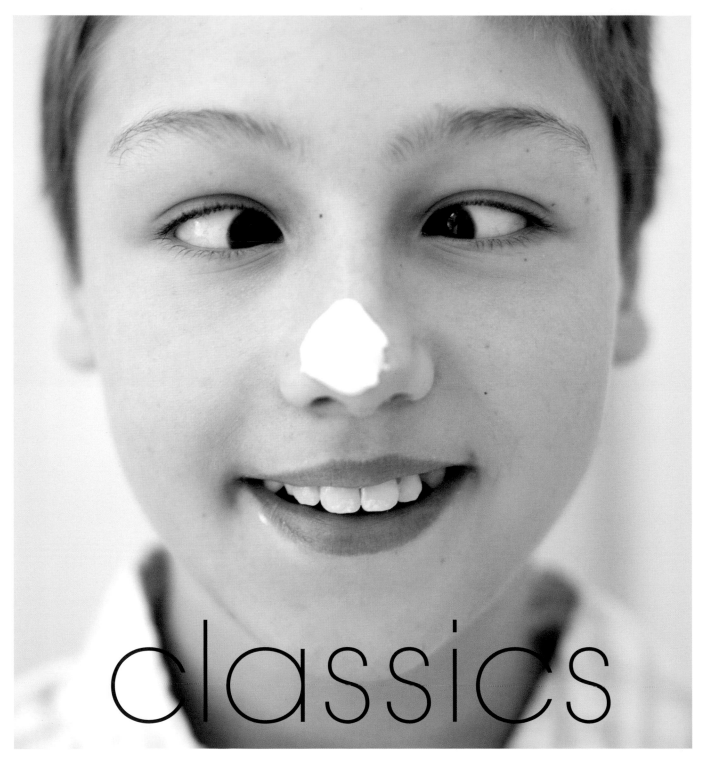

classics

Crisp Bread

Home baked crisp bread is a lot easier to make than you might think. Use baking pans or cookie cutters to make the crisp bread extra special.

50 pieces
You'll need:
¼ **PACKAGE** OF YEAST
2 **CUPS** MILK
1 **TBSP** HONEY
1 ⁹⁄₁₀ **CUPS** COARSE RYE FLOUR
3 ³⁄₅ **CUPS** GRAHAM FLOUR
½ **TBSP** SALT
⅘ **CUPS** FLOUR FOR THE BAKING
    SURFACE
⅖ **CUP** SESAME SEEDS, ⅕ **CUP** FLAX
    SEEDS, AND 1 **TBSP** FLAKE SALT

1. Crumble the yeast into a bowl.

2. **Pour the milk** over the yeast in the bowl, and stir with a spoon or a spatula until the yeast has dissolved.

3. **Add the rest of the ingredients,** except for the wheat flour and the topping, into the bowl. Stir them into a smooth dough. The dough will be sticky.

4. **Cover the dough with plastic,** and place it in the fridge for at least 1 hour.

5. Meanwhile, mix seeds and flake salt in a bowl.

6. **Sprinkle your baking table** with the wheat flour, unwrap the dough from the plastic, and place it on the table.

7. **Roll out the dough** until it is about 1/10-inch thick.

8. Preheat the oven to 400 degrees.

9. **Cover a few baking trays** with parchment paper.

10. **Use cookie cutters, or a knife,** to cut the crisp bread into different shapes.

11. **Place the pieces onto the baking trays** with the parchment paper.

12. **Use a spray bottle** to spray water over the dough pieces so that they become moist. Sprinkle the breads with the seed mix and carefully press them into the dough using a rolling pin.

13. **Place one baking tray at a time** in the middle of the oven and bake the breads about 7 minutes, until they are hard and crispy.

14. **Remove the baking trays** and allow the crisp bread to cool. Store them in a beautiful jar.

54 crisp bread

CINNAMON BUNS

The wonderful smell of freshly baked cinnamon buns beats most things.

1. **Crumble the yeast** into a bowl

2. **Melt the butter** in a pot.

3. **Measure the milk** and pour it into the pot. Heat the liquid until it is 98.6 degrees (lukewarm).

4. **Pour about ⅖ of a cup of the liquid over the yeast** in the bowl, and mix with a spoon until the yeast has dissolved.

5. **Add sugar, salt, cardamom,** and flour to the bowl, and mix them with the liquid into a smooth dough. Knead the dough for 8 minutes by hand, or for 6 minutes if you are using a bread machine.

6. **Cover the bowl with a clean kitchen towel** and allow the dough to rise for 30 minutes.

7. **Sprinkle flour over the baking table** and place the dough on it. Cut the dough into 2 equal parts with a knife.

8. **Roll each part into a rectangle** that is about ¼-inch thick. Spread butter over both rectangles with a wide knife, and sprinkle them with sugar, cinnamon and vanilla sugar. Roll the rectangles into rolls and cut 20 pieces out of each roll.

9. **Transfer the buns to baking cups** and place them on baking sheets and allow them to rise for 45 minutes.

10. **Heat the oven to 475 degrees.**

11. **Crack an egg into a cup** and whisk the egg with a fork. Use a bread brush to carefully brush the buns with the whisked egg. Sprinkle some crushed sugar onto each bun.

12. **Place one baking sheet at a time** in the middle of the oven and bake for about 8 minutes, until the buns have a nice color. Remove the plate and cover the cinnamon buns with a kitchen towel while they cool. Store them in plastic bags.

7.

About 40 buns
You'll need:
1.8 OZ YEAST FOR SWEET DOUGH
5.3 OZ BUTTER
2 CUPS MILK
⅖ CUP GRANULATED SUGAR
½ TSP SALT
½ TSP GROUND CARDAMOM
ABOUT 6 CUPS FLOUR
⅕ CUP FLOUR FOR THE BAKING SURFACE
BAKING CUPS
1 EGG FOR BRUSHING
CRUSHED SUGAR FOR GARNISH

filling:
5.3 OZ BUTTER (ROOM TEMPERATURE)
⅗ CUP GRANULATED SUGAR
3 TBSP CINNAMON
2 TSP VANILLA SUGAR

8.

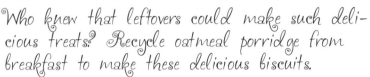

Who knew that leftovers could make such delicious treats? Recycle oatmeal porridge from breakfast to make these delicious biscuits.

oatmeal biscuits

1. **Crumble the yeast into a bowl.** Melt the butter in a pan. Carefully measure the milk and pour it into the pan. Heat the liquid to 98.6 degrees (lukewarm).

2. **Pour the liquid over the yeast in the bowl** and stir with a wooden spoon until the yeast has dissolved.

3. **Pour the oatmeal into the bowl.**

4. **Measure the salt** and the syrup, and pour them into the bowl. Mix thoroughly.

5. **Measure the flour** and add it to the bowl, and mix.

6. **Knead the dough** for at least 10 minutes by hand, or for 8 minutes if you are using a bread machine. Cover the bowl with a kitchen towel and allow the dough to rise for 20 minutes.

7. **Sprinkle flour over the baking surface,** and place the dough on it. Knead the dough for 2 minutes.

8. **Place the dough back into the bowl.** Cover it with a kitchen towel and allow the dough to rise for 20 minutes again.

9. **Preheat the oven to 400 degrees.**

10. **Make the pot biscuits** by dividing the dough into 5 equal parts and then divide each part into 5 equal pieces again so that you will end up with 25 equal pieces. Roll the pieces into balls and carefully press them into the pots that you have buttered and dusted with flour. Cover with a kitchen towel and allow the biscuits to rise for 25 minutes. Place the pots on 2 baking sheets, and

place them in the center of the oven. Bake about 8 minutes, until the biscuits are golden brown.

11. **Make the biscuits** by first dividing the dough into 4 equal parts and then divide each part into 5 equal pieces. Roll each piece into a round ball and place the balls on two baking sheets that have been covered with parchment paper. Cover them with a kitchen towel and allow the dough to rise for 25 minutes. Place one baking sheet at a time in the middle of the oven and bake for 10 minutes.

12. **Allow the biscuits to cool** under a kitchen towel and store them in plastic bags. Remove the biscuits from the pots if you want to freeze them.

20 Biscuits
You'll need:
1.8 OZ YEAST
1.8 OZ BUTTER
1 ¾ CUPS MILK
1 ⅓ CUPS COLD OATMEAL
1 ½ TSP SALT
2 TBSP DARK SYRUP
⅘ CUP GRAHAM FLOUR
5 CUPS FLOUR

Cakes

Cake parties are a lot of fun and can be enjoyed all the time as everyone has a favorite cake so the variations are endless. Chocolate cake, marzipan cake, and strawberry shortcake are just a few of the most popular favor-

Cake Bottom for the Shortcake and the Marzipan Cake

You'll need:

- LARGE EGGS
- CUP GRANULATED SUGAR
- CUP POTATO FLOUR
- CUP FLOUR
- TSP BAKING POWDER
- ½ TBSP WARM WATER

1. Preheat the oven to 350 degrees.

2. Crack the eggs open into a cup. Transfer the eggs to a bowl.

3. Measure the sugar and pour it into the bowl.

4. Take out another bowl. Measure the potato flour, flour, and the baking powder, and pour them into the bowl. Mix with a spoon.

5. Place a sieve over the bowl with the whisked eggs and sift the flour mix through it so that you won't get any lumps in your batter.

6. Measure the water and pour it into the batter. Carefully stir again.

7. Grease and flour a springform pan with a removable bottom, about 9.5 inches in diameter. Pour the batter into the pan.

8. Place the pan on a wire rack in the middle of the oven and bake for 35 minutes. Make sure that the cake does not get burned.

9. Remove the pan from the oven and turn the cake out of the mold onto a plate. Allow it to cool off before you decorate the cake.

Cake Bottom for the Chocolate Cake

You'll need:

- LARGE EGGS
- CUP GRANULATED SUGAR
- CUP POTATO FLOUR
- BSP FLOUR
- SP BAKING POWDER
- SP CACAO POWDER
- TBSP WARM WATER

1. Preheat the oven to 350 degrees.

2. Crack the eggs into a cup and transfer them to a bowl.

3. Measure the sugar and pour it into the bowl. Whisk using an electric mixer until you have a light and fluffy batter.

4. Take out a bowl and measure the potato flour, flour, baking powder, and cacao powder, and pour them into the bowl. Mix with a spoon.

5. Place a sieve over the bowl with the fluffy egg batter and sift the flour mix through it to prevent lumps in the batter. Carefully stir with a spatula.

6. Measure the water and add it to the batter. Carefully stir again.

7. Grease and flour a springform pan with a removable bottom, about 9.5 inches in diameter. Pour the batter into the pan.

8. Place the pan on a wire rack in the middle of the oven and bake for 35 minutes. Make sure not to burn the cake.

9. Remove the pan from the oven and turn the cake over onto a plate. Allow it to cool off before you decorate the cake.

7.

Choose how to fill and decorate your cake according to your taste. The possibilities are endless!

cakes **61**

strawberry
shortcake

**Filling and Decoration
You'll need:**
⅘ **CUP** VANILLA CREAM
⅘ **CUP** STRAWBERRY JAM
2 CUPS WHIPPED CREAM
FRESH STRAWBERRIES

2.

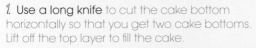

1. Use a long knife to cut the cake bottom horizontally so that you get two cake bottoms. Lift off the top layer to fill the cake.

2. Spread vanilla cream and strawberry jam over the bottom layer of the cake bottom. Cover it with the top layer of the cake bottom and spread whipped cream on top and around the cake bottom. Then decorate the cake with whipped cream in a nice pattern, and fresh strawberries.

1. Use a long knife to divide the cake bottom horizontally into two pieces. Lift off the top layer to fill the cake.

2. Spread vanilla cream and whipped cream on top of the bottom cake layer. Add the top layer of the cake bottom and spread whipped cream on top and on the sides of the cake. Decorate the middle of the top of the cake with whipped cream. Decorate with chocolate whipped cream around the edges. You can also garnish the sides with grated dark chocolate. Use a sieve to dust some cacao powder over the cake. Garnish with raspberries.

Chocolate Cake

Filling and Garnish

You'll need:

⅘ CUP VANILLA CREAM
1 ⅓ CUPS + 1 ⅓ CUPS WHIPPING
   CREAM
1.8 OZ DARK CHOCOLATE
1 TBSP CACAO POWDER
FRESH RASPBERRIES

CHOCOLATE CREAM

1. Use an electric whisk to beat the whipping cream.

2. Melt little pieces of dark chocolate in a small bowl in the microwave. Allow it to cool off a little.

3. Pour the melted chocolate into the whipped cream and carefully stir with a spatula.

Marzipan Cake

Filling and Garnish

You'll need:

⅘ CUP VANILLA CREAM
1 ⅓ CUPS WHIPPED CREAM
COLORED MARZIPAN

1. **Use a long knife** to cut the cake bottom horizontally into two pieces. Leave the pieces stacked on top of each other, and cut the cake into the desired shape. You can make a funny looking creature, a ladybug, or even a spaceship. When you are done cutting the shape, lift off the top piece to fill the cake.

2. **Spread vanilla cream and whipped cream** on the bottom piece. Place the other piece on top and spread whipped cream on top and on the sides of both pieces.

3. **Use a rolling pin to flatten the marzipan into a piece that you place on top of the cake.** Cut or shape marzipan into pieces for garnish.

You'll need:

- **3.5 OZ** BUTTER
- **²/₅ CUP** GRANULATED SUGAR
- **²/₅ CUP** OATS
- **¾ CUP** WHEAT FLOUR
- **1 PINCH** OF SALT
- LEMON ZEST FROM 1 LEMON
- **⁴/₅ CUP** CHOPPED RHUBARB
- **1 BOX** OF FRESH STRAWBERRIES, ABOUT 8.8 OZ
- **1 TSP** POTATO FLOUR

CRUMB PIE

Enjoy your favorite berries and fruits in this delicious pie. We decided to add some rhubarb (which really is a vegetable) and strawberries for a tasty, sweet, and zesty combination.

1. Preheat the oven to 425 degrees.

2. Measure the butter, sugar, oats, flour, and salt, and pour them into a bowl. Add the lemon zest. Mix quickly with your hands, or with a fork, until you have a crumbly mass.

3. Take out a pie dish that is about 9.5 inches in diameter and fill it with rhubarb and strawberries. Sprinkle potato flour over the filling and mix.

4. Spread the crumbs over the rhubarb and the strawberries and place the pie dish on a wire rack in the middle of the oven. Bake the pie for 20 minutes until it is golden brown and the fruit bubbles a bit along the pie edge.

5. Remove the pie from the oven and allow it to cool a little. Serve it while it is still a bit warm, with vanilla sauce or ice cream.

GRATING THE LEMON ZEST
Use the fine side of the grater. Make sure that you only grate the outer, yellow layer of the lemon. The white layer is bitter and will not add a nice flavor to the cake.

This recipe is a little bit more difficult and requires an adult to help you out. However, it ends in plenty of delicious graham biscuits well worth the process!

1. Crumble the yeast into a bowl.

2. Add the honey and the butter into a pan, and melt it.

3. Measure the milk and pour it into the pan. Heat the liquid to about 98.6 degrees (lukewarm).

4. Pour about ⅖ cup of the liquid into the bowl with the yeast and stir with a wooden spoon until the yeast has dissolved.

5. Pour the rest of the liquid into the bowl and stir a little.

6. Measure the rest of the ingredients and pour them into the bowl. Mix and knead into a dough, 10 minutes by hand, or 8 minutes in a bread machine.

7. Cover the bowl with a clean kitchen towel and allow the dough to rise for 30 minutes.

8. Butter 2 baking sheets.

9. Sprinkle a little bit of flour onto the baking table and place the dough on top.

10. Knead the dough for a little bit before you use a knife to divide it into 4 equal pieces. Cut each piece into 6 equal parts so that you end up with 24 pieces. Shape the pieces into oval biscuits.

11. Place the biscuits onto the baking sheets and cover them with clean kitchen towels. Allow the biscuits to rise for 15 minutes.

12. Meanwhile, preheat the oven to 425 degrees.

13. Place one baking sheet at a time in the middle of the oven and bake the biscuits for 15 minutes.

14. Remove the baking sheets from the oven and place them on the stove. Allow them to cool for a few minutes so that you can touch the biscuits without burning your fingers.

15. Divide each biscuit with a fork by sticking it into the biscuit all around. Now, the biscuits need to roast in the oven. Preheat the oven to 425-475 degrees. Place the biscuits onto the baking sheets with the cut-side facing up. You might need to use the baking sheets several times to fit all the biscuits on them.

16. Place the baking sheets in the middle of the oven for 6 minutes so that the biscuits get a little bit of color. Then lower the heat to 200 degrees and keep the oven door open slightly. Dry the biscuits in the oven for about 2 1/2 hours.

17. Store the biscuits in a beautiful jar.

Graham Biscuits

About 48 biscuits
You'll need:
- 1.8 OZ YEAST
- 3.5 OZ BUTTER
- 4 TBSP HONEY
- 2 CUPS MILK
- 2 TSP SALT
- 1 ½ TBSP GROUND CARDAMOM
- 3 ⅖ CUPS GRAHAM FLOUR
- 1 ⁹/₁₀ CUPS FLOUR

About 15 Scones
You'll need:
1 ⅓ **CUPS** FLOUR
⅘ **CUP** GRAHAM FLOUR
2 **TSP** BAKING POWDER
½ **TSP** SALT
1.8 **OZ** BUTTER
⅘ **CUP** MILK

This is a quick bread that does not require any yeast. Use cookie cutters to create fun shapes.

Scones

1. Measure the flour, baking powder, and salt, and transfer them to a bowl.

2. Put the butter in the bowl and quickly mix it into a crumbly mass. You can use a ladle.

3. Measure the milk and pour it into the bowl. Mix the dough with your hands. Don't work it too long—or it will become tough.

4. Sprinkle the baking table with flour, and transfer the dough to it. Carefully roll it out with a rolling pin so that it is about 1-inch thick.

5. Use cookie cutters to create shapes for the scones.

6. Preheat the oven to 475 degrees.

7. Place the scones on parchment paper on 2 baking sheets, and place them in the center of the oven. Bake for about 10 minutes, until the scones have gotten a little bit of color. Remove the baking sheets from the oven and allow the scones to cool before you serve them.

8. Scones are tastier when they are freshly baked, but you can store them in plastic bags for a few days. Serve with butter or lemon curd.

Tip! You do not need to use cookie cutters to shape the scones. You can use a knife to cut out squares or triangles. You can also make two big cakes out of the dough.

Dish Towel

Spatula

LE CREUSET

Bowl

Rolling

Teaspoon (tsp)

Bread Brush

Tablespoon (tbsp)

1/2 Cup

Cake Tester

Cutting Board

Measuring Cup

Wooden
Spoon

1/4 teaspoon

Electric
Mixer

CONVERSION CHARTS

METRIC AND IMPERIAL CONVERSIONS
(These conversions are rounded for convenience)

Ingredient	Cups/Tablespoons/Teaspoons	Ounces	Grams/Milliliters
Butter	1 cup = 16 tablespoons = 2 sticks	8 ounces	230 grams
Cheese, shredded	1 cup	4 ounces	110 grams
Cream cheese	1 tablespoon	0.5 ounce	14.5 grams
Cornstarch	1 tablespoon	0.3 ounce	8 grams
Flour, all-purpose	1 cup/1 tablespoon	4.5 ounces/0.3 ounce	125 grams/8 grams
Flour, whole wheat	1 cup	4 ounces	120 grams
Fruit, dried	1 cup	4 ounces	120 grams
Fruits or veggies, chopped	1 cup	5 to 7 ounces	145 to 200 grams
Fruits or veggies, puréed	1 cup	8.5 ounces	245 grams
Honey, maple syrup, or corn syrup	1 tablespoon	0.75 ounce	20 grams
Liquids: cream, milk, water, or juice	1 cup	8 fluid ounces	240 milliliters
Oats	1 cup	5.5 ounces	150 grams
Salt	1 teaspoon	0.2 ounce	6 grams
Spices: cinnamon, cloves, ginger, or nutmeg (ground)	1 teaspoon	0.2 ounce	5 milliliters
Sugar, brown, firmly packed	1 cup	7 ounces	200 grams
Sugar, white	1 cup/1 tablespoon	7 ounces/0.5 ounce	200 grams/12.5 grams
Vanilla extract	1 teaspoon	0.2 ounce	4 grams

OVEN TEMPERATURES

Fahrenheit	Celsius	Gas Mark
225°	110°	¼
250°	120°	½
275°	140°	1
300°	150°	2
325°	160°	3
350°	180°	4
375°	190°	5
400°	200°	6
425°	220°	7
450°	230°	8